WHAT IS ART?

Sculpture

KAREN HOSACK

CHICAGO, ILLINOIS

Customer Service 888-454-2279
Visit our website at www.heinemannraintree.com

Editorial: Adam Miller, Charlotte Guillain, Clare Lewis,
and Catherine Veitch
Design: Victoria Bevan and AMR Design Ltd
Illustrations: David Woodroffe
Picture Research: Mica Brancic
and Helen Reilly/Arnos Design Ltd
Production: Victoria Fitzgerald

Originated by Modern Age
Printed and bound by CTPS (China Translation and
Printing Services Ltd)

13 12 11 10 09
10 9 8 7 6 5 4 3 2 1

Library of Congress Cataloging-in-Publication Data
Hosack, Karen.
  Sculpture / Karen Hosack.
    p. cm. -- (What is art?)
  Includes bibliographical references and index.
  ISBN 978-1-4109-3161-0 (hc)
  1. Sculpture--Juvenile literature. I. Title.
  NB1143.H67 2008
  730--dc22
                                  2008009727

Acknowledgments
The publishers would like to thank the following for
permission to reproduce photographs:
©AKG p. **19** (Robert O Dea); ©Andy Goldworthy p. **12**;
©The Bridgeman Art Library pp. **6** (Christie's Images),
17 (© Succession Marcel Duchamp/ADAGP, Paris and
DACS, London 2008), © DACS /Vera & Arturo Schwarz
Collection of Dada and Surrealist Art), **22** (Private
Collection), **27** (Private Collection, Photo © Christie's
Images); ©Corbis pp. **4** (Gianni Dagli Orti), **5** (Francis
G. Mayer), **14** (Jason Hawkes), **18** (Mike McQueen),
21 (Kieran Doherty/Reuters), **24** (Richard Cummins),
26 (Sandy Felsenthal); ©Gerard Scarfe p. **25**; ©Getty
Images p. **20** (The Image Bank/IC Productions);
©Hawaiian State foundation of Culture and Arts/Satoru
Abe East and West 1971 p. **11**; ©istockphoto p. **13**
(Sami Suni); ©Martin Creed p. **16**; ©Rex Features p.
8 (Dazed & Confused); ©Copyright Estate of Robert
Smithson, Courtesy James Cohan Gallery, New York
p. **9**; ©Scala Archives p. **10** (Museum of Modern Art
(MoMA)); ©Scala pp. **15** (Photo Art Media/HIP/Scala,
Florence), **23** (Digital image, The Museum of Modern
Art, New York/Scala, Florence); ©Werner Foreman
Archives p. **7**.

Cover photograph of Auguste Rodin's hand study in
plaster. Plaster hands, a study molded by Auguste
Rodin, are displayed at the Musée Rodin in Paris,
reproduced with permission of Corbis/Bob Krist.

Every effort has been made to contact copyright
holders of any material reproduced in this book.
Any omissions will be rectified in subsequent
printings if notice is given to the publishers.

Contents

Any words appearing in the text in bold, **like this**,
are explained in the glossary.

What Is Sculpture?

A sculpture is usually **three-dimensional**. Paintings and photographs are flat, but you can often move around a sculpture. You can see it from different sides and may also be able to touch it.

Children make three-dimensional models from an early age. It seems natural for people to make shapes out of materials they find around them, such as sand, mud, or clay. You might have made some yourself, perhaps from play dough or even with your food when you were younger!

Discobolos, after a bronze statue by Myron, c. 450 BCE

This Roman copy of a Greek sculpture was made over 2,450 years ago. It shows a man throwing a discus, which was a very popular sport at the time.

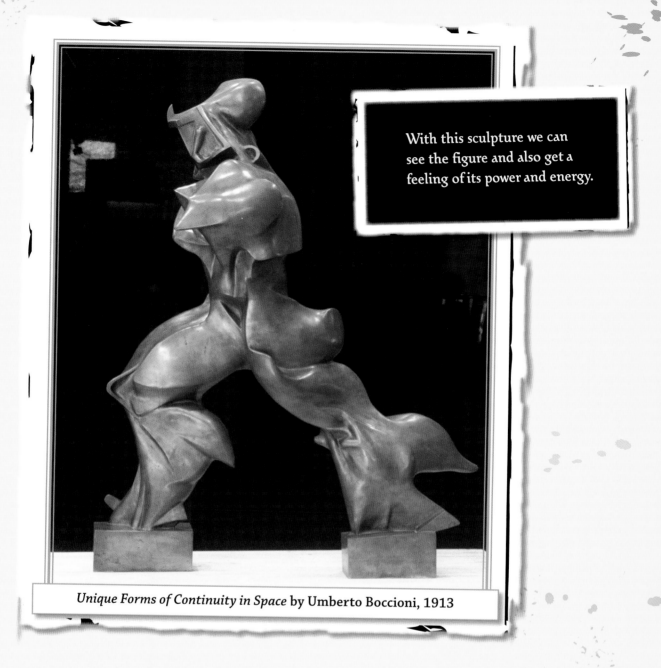

With this sculpture we can see the figure and also get a feeling of its power and energy.

Unique Forms of Continuity in Space by Umberto Boccioni, 1913

Both of these sculptures show movement. The sculpture of the discus thrower is carved from a hard material called **marble** and is more than 4 feet (1.2 meters) tall. The sculpture is very heavy and still, but the forward motion is clear, and it looks as if the figure is almost real.

The other sculpture was made less than 100 years ago. The figure is walking, and it looks as though it is pushing into the wind. The artist has included what he thinks the force of the wind might look like.

Looking at Sculpture

You might think that you do not know much about sculpture, but if you ask a few questions about what you see, you can enjoy looking at it. A good place to start is thinking about why someone might have made the sculpture. What do you think the artist was trying to tell us with the piece of sculpture below?

Look at this very famous sculpture. You can probably guess that the figure is thinking deeply about something. In fact this sculpture is called *The Thinker*. What might the person be thinking about?

The Thinker by Auguste Rodin, 1880

This mask was used for special occassions. How do you think it would feel to wear it?

Angolan dance mask, 19th century

This beautifully made mask was created to be worn in dance ceremonies. Masks are often used in rituals and for **spiritual** purposes. People all over the world often make sculptures to celebrate their beliefs. Can you think of any examples of this?

Finding Clues

When you get to know some information about a sculpture, it will help you to explore it more fully. Try to find out what the sculpture is made from. Then think about what this can tell you.

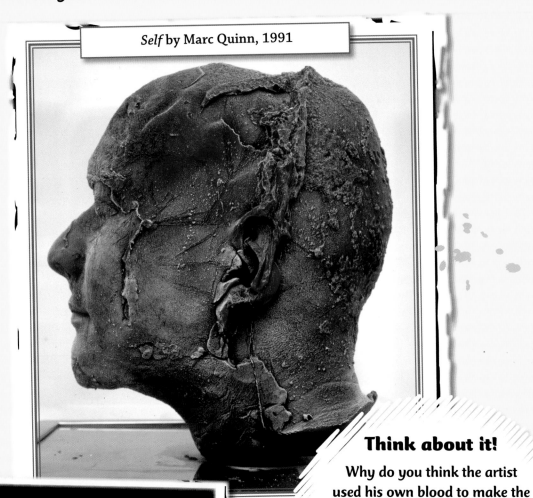

Self by Marc Quinn, 1991

This is a self-portrait of the artist. It is a **cast** of the artist's head made of 9 pints of his own blood. The blood was frozen and kept refrigerated in a special display case.

Think about it!

Why do you think the artist used his own blood to make the sculpture? Warm blood flows around a living person, but here it is cold and still. Every person's blood has **genetic** information in it. Would it make a difference if the blood had come from another person, or even an animal?

Spiral Jetty by Robert Smithson, 1970

In the Great Salt Lake of Utah, there is a sculpture that is made from huge rocks. The artist used 6,650 tons of rocks to construct the giant **spiral**, which is 1,500 feet (460 meters) long. The fact that it is made from natural objects in the open air and is a natural spiral shape means that the sculpture looks as if it is growing out of the **environment**.

Natural Inspiration

Many sculptors are inspired by nature. Look carefully at this mobile. Do the shapes remind you of anything? This time the title of the sculpture does not help you. Think about how the shapes might move in the wind. What words might you use to describe this—"floating," perhaps, or "gliding"? There are no right or wrong answers. Art can mean different things to different people.

Untitled by Alexander Calder, 1939

If the shapes were supposed to be animals, what might they be?

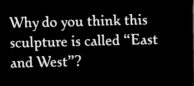

Why do you think this sculpture is called "East and West"?

East and West by Satoru Abe, 1971

This sculpture is more clearly based on a particular natural form. The sculptor, Satoru Abe, is famous for using the **symbol** of a tree in his work. Think about what trees can stand for. They have roots that hold them in the ground. They have strong trunks that branch off and grow upward toward the light. How would you describe this tree sculpture?

How Long Do Sculptures Last?

Sometimes artists decide to make sculptures from materials that they know will not last very long at all. This colorful piece is made from the leaves of a rowan tree. The artist has carefully sorted the leaves into their different colors and then placed them in position. He then took a photograph, so we can see a record of the sculpture long after the wind and rain have made the sculpture disappear.

Rowan Leaves with a Hole by Andy Goldsworthy, 1987

How long do you think this sculpture might last?

Liberty Enlightening the World, or *The Statue of Liberty*, built in 1886

The seven rays on the crown represent the seven continents, and the torch is a shining light of hope.

The sculpture above was designed to last a very long time. The French and American people built the *Statue of Liberty* to celebrate the centennial (100th anniversary) of the **Declaration of Independence**. The statue is a **symbol** of freedom to millions of people all over the world and an important work of **engineering**. It was made in 300 separate pieces, and the main body of the statue was shipped across the Atlantic Ocean and finally put together in New York Harbor in July 1886—10 years after the centennial.

Sculpture and Symbolism

The Princess of Wales Memorial Fountain in London, England, celebrates the life of Princess Diana. The water sculpture is a large oval ring made of granite. It is 690 feet (210 meters) long, with grass in the center where children can play. Water flows from two different directions and at different speeds, and this makes areas that bubble softly and others that are more rapid. The artist wanted to show how the princess's life was sometimes complicated and dramatic, and at other times it was more calm and peaceful.

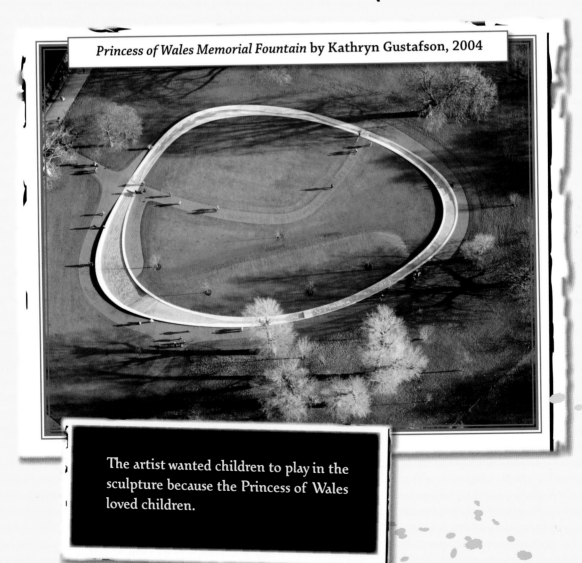

Princess of Wales Memorial Fountain by Kathryn Gustafson, 2004

The artist wanted children to play in the sculpture because the Princess of Wales loved children.

Art and war

World War I (1914–1918) was the first war to use mechanical weapons, such as machine guns and tanks. These machines were able to kill from great distances. Soldiers operating these weapons might not even know how many people they killed. Many artists, such as Jacob Epstein, tried to show the downsides to the age of machines.

Can you see what the figure is protecting inside?

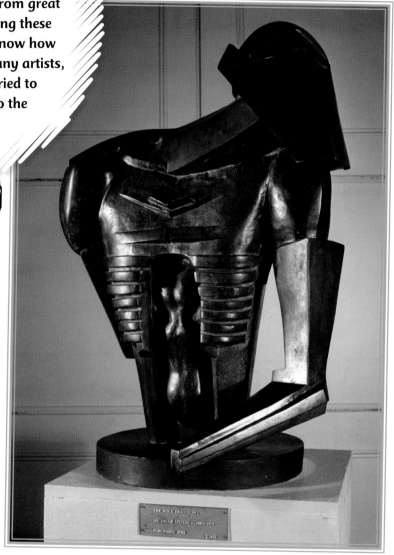

The Rock Drill by Jacob Epstein, 1913–1914

The symbolism of the sculpture above is very powerful. Look carefully and ask yourself what you are looking at. Can you see a head or arms? It looks more like a cross between an animal and a machine than a human being. The sculpture makes us ask questions about what it is to be human during a difficult time. The artist made it at the time of political unrest in Europe before **World War I**.

Found Objects

Is this a sculpture or just a ball of crumpled-up paper? Can it possibly be both? Sculptures like this make us think about what art really is. Can art be made from any materials? The answer is yes. So, what turns this ball of paper into a work of art? Is it just because it is displayed as art? Could it be because the artist who made it called it art?

A Sheet of A4 Paper Crumpled into a Ball by Martin Creed, 1995

The point of this sculpture might be to make us think about what art is. Do you think the artist has succeeded?

Fountain by Marcel Duchamp, 1917

Do you recognize this object? You are more likely to if you are
a boy! It is a urinal that is usually found in a men's public bathroom.
The artist wanted to make people really think about what art is.
He wanted people to see that art did not always have to involve the
skill of making things well. He thought it could be about different
viewpoints. With this sculpture, all he has done is taken an everyday
object and given it a title. He also signed it with a fake name.

For Whom Was It Made?

When we know for whom a sculpture was made, it can help us to understand the meaning of the work. These figures were made for Chinese Emperor Qin Shi in 210–209 BCE. They were buried with him to help him rule another empire in the **afterlife**. The public was never supposed to see them. In 1974 a farmer found the figures when he was drilling for water. The figures are now known as the Terracotta Army.

The Terracotta Army of Emperor Qin Shi, c. 210 BCE

There are over 6,000 larger-than-life figures of soldiers and horses in the Terracotta Army.

The artist wanted this sculpture to be a **symbol** of love, warmth, and happiness. Or did he?

Puppy by Jeff Koons, 1997

This is a piece of sculpture that the public is definitely supposed to see. The 40-foot- (12-meter-) tall sculpture is made of steel, soil, and flowers. It has been shown outside various public buildings all over the world. Many people enjoy this huge, lovable sculpture, with its cute name and beautiful flowers. The artist wanted to make people happy, but could he also be poking fun at the world of art?

Huge Sculptures

The public is supposed to get fully involved with both of these sculptures. *Cloud Gate* is a 110-ton stainless steel sculpture in Millennium Park, in Chicago. It has a 12-foot- (4-meter-) high arch under it, a bit like a gateway. People can wander underneath the sculpture and see reflections of themselves, the city skyline, and the clouds. The images they see are constantly changing.

Cloud Gate by Anish Kapoor, 2004

Cloud Gate is one of the largest sculptures in the world. It is 66 feet (20 meters) long and 33 feet (10 meters) high. What do you think people's reactions to this sculpture might be?

Walking inside this sculpture is strange because you do not know which direction you are going. Why do you think the artist wanted this?

Blind Light by Antony Gormley, 2007

Blind Light is a sculpture that people can wander inside. It is a large glass box that can fit up to 25 people at one time. Inside, you cannot see anyone else because there is thick **water vapor** filling the air. It can be hard to find your way out! People inside the sculpture look like part of the art from the outside.

Look Again!

At first the meaning of a sculpture might not be clear, but it is always a good idea to look again.

Abstract art can be difficult to understand at first. It is often open to lots of different interpretations. What does this sculpture say to you?

Two Piece Reclining Figure: Bust by Henry Moore, 1975

These two pieces look like smooth, pebble-like shapes placed together. Could they be anything else? Could they represent, or stand for, something? If so, what might they represent? The artist Henry Moore simplified the shapes he saw in the human body. We call these sculptures **abstract** because they are taken from an original **source**, but have been changed into something else.

Surreal

Meret Oppenheim was considered a Surrealist. That meant that she tried to create works that were more dream-like than real. Surrealist art was never logical or easy to understand. Different people can look at a Surrealist work of art and come up with very different ideas of what it might mean.

> Would you want to drink from this cup?

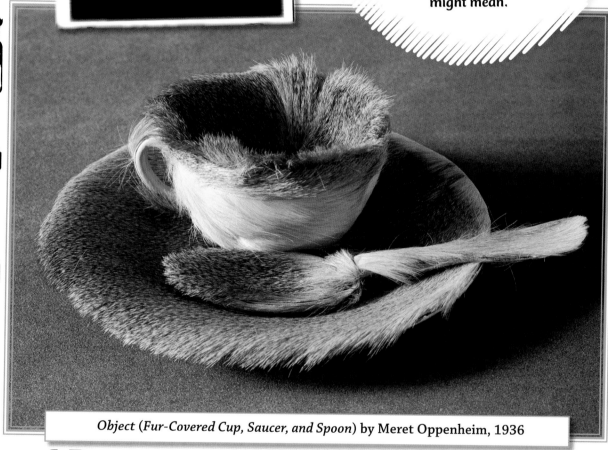

Object (Fur-Covered Cup, Saucer, and Spoon) by Meret Oppenheim, 1936

This is an everyday set of objects, including a cup, saucer, and spoon. The odd thing is that they seem to be made out of fur. The original source of this sculpture is very clear, but the artist has changed the meaning of the ordinary objects by using totally unsuitable materials. What is the point of a cup that cannot be used? Where else might you find such odd ideas? In dreams, perhaps?

The Unexpected

Some sculptures look straightforward to begin with, but then have an unexpected twist. This sculpture is of a spoon and a cherry, which would be a very ordinary sight in a kitchen. But the sculpture is in a park in Minneapolis, Minnesota, and is the size of a bus! What would you think if you stumbled on this sculpture when you were out for a walk?

Spoonbridge and Cherry by Claes Oldenburg, 1985–88

Spoonbridge and Cherry is a fountain sculpture. It stretches across a small pond, and a stream of water flows over the cherry.

Think about it!

The sculptor who created *Spoonbridge and Cherry* once said, "Very often I am sitting at dinner and I take out my notebook. I get very inspired when I eat, for some reason."

Chairman Mao by Gerald Scarfe, 1971

This is a lighthearted sculpture made by an artist who is famous for looking at world leaders in his work. Here he plays with the meaning of the word "chairman." A chairman is a person who leads a meeting or a group of people. The artist has used the word literally by actually shaping a chair into the image of a man. In this case the man is Chairman Mao, who was a leader of China in the 20th century.

Exploring Sculpture

In this book we have looked at many different sculptures. Some have been small, others huge. Some have been made from traditional materials, such as **marble** and clay. Other sculptures have been made from found objects, and even the artist's own blood. We have thought about what artists might be trying to say in their work, but we have also thought about what the pieces might mean to us personally.

Art is very powerful and can encourage strong reactions from individuals. This can be clearly seen when a piece of public sculpture is put in a place where people often visit.

Untitled by Pablo Picasso, Daley Plaza, Chicago, 1967

What would you think if this large work of art were put in a place near where you live?

Little Dancer, Aged 14 by Edgar Degas, 1881

Less **abstract** sculptures can sometimes appeal to people more because they can easily recognize the subject. It is important to try to give all art some time and thought. You might discover something in an abstract sculpture that you did not see at first. You do not have to like everything, but with an open mind you might be pleasantly surprised and find something new and interesting!

Timeline

c. 450 BCE	Discobolos, Roman **marble** copy after a bronze statue by Myron (p. 4)
c. 210–209 BCE	The Terracotta Army of Emperor Qin Shi is buried (p. 18)
c. 1800s CE	Dance Mask, Angola, Africa (p. 7)
1880	Auguste Rodin, *The Thinker* (p. 6)
1881	Edgar Degas, *Little Dancer, Aged 14* (p. 27)
1886	*The Statue of Liberty*, New York, New York (p. 13)
1913	Umberto Boccioni, *Unique Forms of Continuity in Space* (p. 5)
1913	Jacob Epstein, *The Rock Drill* (p. 15)
1917	Marcel Duchamp, *Fountain* (p. 17)
1936	Meret Oppenheim, *Object (Fur-Covered Cup, Saucer, and Spoon)* (p. 23)
1939	Alexander Calder, *Untitled* (p. 10)
1967	Pablo Picasso, *Untitled*, Chicago, Daley Plaza (p. 26)
1970	Robert Smithson, *Spiral Jetty*, Great Salt Lake, Utah (p. 9)
1971	Satoru Abe, *East and West* (p. 11)
	Gerald Scarfe, *Chairman Mao* (p. 25)
1975	Henry Moore, *Two Piece Reclining Figure: Bust* (p. 22)
1987	Andy Goldsworthy, *Rowan Leaves with a Hole* (p. 12)
1985–88	Claes Oldenburg, *Spoonbridge and Cherry* (p. 24)
1991	Marc Quinn, *Self* (p. 8)
1995	Martin Creed, *A Sheet of A4 Paper Crumpled into a Ball* (p. 16)
1997	Jeff Koons, *Puppy* (p. 19)
2004	Kathryn Gustafson, *The Princess of Wales Memorial Fountain*, Hyde Park, London (p. 14)
2004	Anish Kapoor, *Cloud Gate*, Millennium Park, Chicago (p. 20)
2007	Antony Gormley, *Blind Light* (p. 21)

Where to See Sculpture

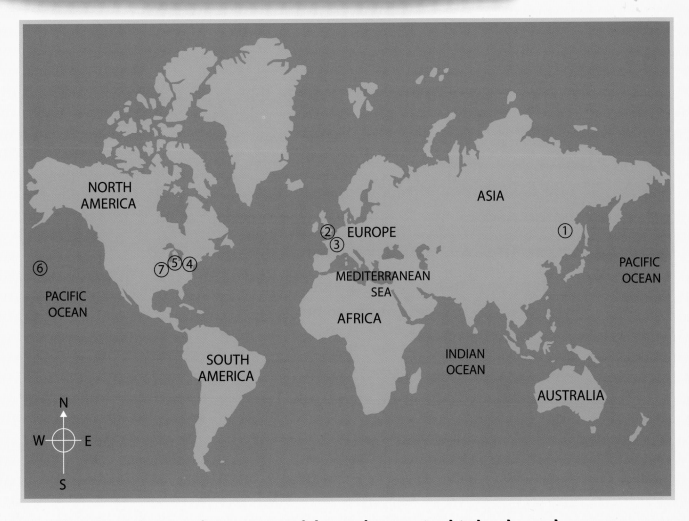

This map shows where some of the sculptures in this book can be seen.

① Shaanxi Province, China
The Terracotta Army

② London, England
British Museum:
Discobolos, after
Myron
The Royal Academy:
*Little Dancer, Aged
Fourteen*, Degas
Tate Britain: Examples of
Moore's work
Hyde Park, London:
Princess of Wales
Memorial Fountain

③ Paris, France
Musée Rodin:
The Thinker, Rodin

④ New York, New York
The Statue of Liberty
Museum of Modern Art:
The Rock Drill, Epstein
Object (Fur-Covered
Cup, Saucer, and
Spoon), Oppenheim

⑤ Chicago, Illinois
Chicago Daley Plaza:
Untitled, Picasso

⑥ Hawaii
Hawaii State Art Museum:
East and West, Abe

⑦ Minneapolis, Minnesota
Minneapolis Sculpture
Garden:
*Spoonbridge and
Cherry*, Oldenburg

Glossary

abstract art not meant to look like real life, but that shows feelings or an idea

afterlife where some people believe people go after death

cast something shaped in a mold

Declaration of Independence document approved on July 4, 1776, that formally separated the United States from British rule

engineering way things are designed and constructed

environment natural and human-made surroundings, in which plants, animals, and people live

genetic information in molecules that make up animals and plants

marble limestone that is highly polished

source where something begins

spiral coiled shape

spiritual relating to the spirit; not physical or of this world

symbol something that represents something else

three-dimensional when an object has height, width, and depth

water vapor moisture from water suspended in the air

World War I war (1914–1918) between the Central Powers (Germany, Austria-Hungary, Turkey, and Bulgaria) and the Allies (Great Britain, France, Russia, Italy, and the United States)

Learn More

Books to read

Civardi, Anne. *What Is a Sculpture?* (*Art's Alive*).
    Mankato, Minn.: Sea to Sea, 2005.

Flux, Paul. *Shape* (*How Artists Use*). Chicago:
    Heinemann Library, 2008.

Spilsbury, Richard. *Sculpture* (*Stories in Art*). New York:
    PowerKids, 2008.

Websites to visit

The website of the Minneapolis Sculpture Garden, which
includes *Spoonbridge and Cherry*

http://garden.walkerart.org

The Metropolitan Museum of Art's website for kids

www.metmuseum.org/explore/museumkids.htm

The National Gallery of Art's website for kids

www.nga.gov/kids/kids.htm

Index